HEREND

HEREND

*Traditional Craftsmanship
in the 20th Century*

Introduction written and illustrations selected by *József Vadas*
Art works photographed by *Károly Szelényi*
Art works captioned by *Vera Varga*
Translated by *Julianna Parti*
Book design by *Judit Löblin*

The book is published by *F. Szelényi House, Veszprém* on behalf of the
Herend Porcelain Manufactory Ltd.

Production by IDG HUNGARY Ltd., Budapest (typesetting),
Stádium Nyomda, Budapest (BW Repro)
Bösmüller Press, Vienna-Budapest (colour separation, printing, binding)

We acknowledge with thanks the help given in preparing this book
by József Kovács, Managing director, by the staff of the Herend Porcelain
Manufactory and Herend Museum and by the staff of the Budapest Museum
of Applied Arts.

Front cover: An ornamental plate.
An authentic replica of an original from the early Fischer period
Back cover: An ornamental vase with a lid, with colour painting and gilding over
the glaze. The scenes are miniatures by Bábur-Náme
Flyleaves: Copper engravings made by István Zádor for the 1939 centenary
exhibition of the Herend Porcelain Factory
Title page: Tête-à-tête service, c. 1890, in the "Tupini" pattern
Page 17: Plate, c. 1880, in the "Miramare" pattern
Page 75: The bird motif of the "Rothschild" pattern

ISBN 963 8155 05 1

Herend and Hungarian porcelain made an important contribution to the rather belated industrial and social development of the country in the 19th century. Back in the reign of King Matthias (1443–1490), Hungary had been one of the great economic and cultural powers in Europe, but that position was lost in the mid–16th century, when the centre of the country was occupied by the Ottoman Empire. Severe damage was suffered under the Turks and in the warfare between the Ottoman and Habsburg empires during the 150 years up to 1699. This set Hungary back by centuries, both economically and socially, so that the rise of the middle class, along with urbanization and industrialization, was postponed until the beginning of the 19th century.

One symptom of backwardness is that this late development came from a curious direction–not from a third estate of commoners, but from an educated petty nobility. These reformers usually had a legal training and held posts in government, while leadership and encouragement came from a handful of enlightened aristocrats who had acquired a modern European outlook.

Two political figures stand out in this surge of development and reform: the aristocrat Count István Széchenyi (1791–1860), and the petty nobleman Lajos Kossuth (1802–1894). Széchenyi made countless seminal contributions; not least he was the first person in Hungary to emphasize the economic necessity of a modern credit system. Kossuth, a prominent reformer in the semi-feudal Diets of the period, became the most influential and effective advocate of bourgeois development and modernization. The changes that they and the other reformers pressed for tied in closely with the establishment of Hungarian industry. They recognized that the prosperity of the country depended on transforming the economic system. Hungary was backward because it was based on a system of great agricultural estates where the system of production was still medieval. Before the country could advance, the serfs had to be freed, modern farming methods introduced, and modern manufacturing

Fischer Moricz Herend 842	HEREND 1843	F.M. 843 HEREND	Herend 844	Herend 846

industry, commerce and finance established. In addition, Hungary had to gain control over its own affairs, for it was still a mere province of the Habsburg Empire, the emperor being the Hungarian king.

That was the background behind the great initiatives taken to promote Hungarian industry, including the first great parade of its products at the Industrial Exhibition of 1842.

So the foundation of Herend and Hungarian porcelain manufacture was part of a wider process. The Hungarian ceramics industry did not arrive out of the blue, of course. With the re-establishment of feudalism after the Turkish period, pottery had grown into an important cottage industry in the 17th and 18th centuries. Centres with their own styles had grown up, particularly on the Great Plain of Central and Eastern Hungary, but there were gilds of potters selling their wares in the towns in many Western Hungarian villages as well, including Herend. This tradition of folk pottery survived until the recent past, because factories developed so late and factory goods remained too expensive for the country's large class of peasantry. Only towards the end of the last century, when the peasant way of life broke down and the factories became capable of producing cheap mass products, did folk pottery go into decline. In fact in certain more isolated communities, dynasties of highly skilled traditional potters survived until the very recent past.

Until the 17th century, porcelain had been imported from China by ship. It took centuries of experiments in Europe before Johann Friedrich Böttger finally discovered how to make it in 1705, and Meissen and the other porcelain factories were established. One of the by-products of the attempts to make porcelain was faience, ware that takes its name from the city of Faenza in Italy. Faience does not match porcelain in its appearance or physical properties, but it approaches it. Faience production spread to Hungary, and the faience workshops in places like Holics, Tata, Pápa and Hollóháza can be considered as milestones in the development of the Hungarian fine ceramics industry and the direct forebears of porcelain making. They made the first experimental pieces of porcelain and trained many craftsmen who later worked in the porcelain factory.

Most of Europe's porcelain factories were founded by monarchs and princes. For centuries porcelain counted as a precious material, and it is symbolic that Böttger, an alchemist seeking gold, should have cracked the secret. Even after the industry became established in Europe, it remained precious because of the special way it was made and decorated. But the porcelain industry in Hungary was founded by an entrepreneur, not a princely court, even though the Hungarian middle class was still in its infancy. Successful attempts to make porcelain took place at a workshop in Herend, a

| *F M*
HEREND
846 | *F M*
HEREND
847 | *à Herendi Porczella*
gyár
HEREND
847 | *M* Herend | |

6

village in the Bakony Hills to the north of Lake Balaton. Herend porcelain, a source of national pride in the last century, remains a sought-after export item to this day.

The beginnings were fraught with difficulties. There had been an imperial porcelain factory in Vienna since 1718, and competition was feared. The manager of the Faenza faience factory was expelled from the country for working in Hungary. An application to set up a porcelain factory from Tivadar Batthyány, a citizen of Pest, was rejected on the grounds that he had too little capital. The pieces he had made were smashed by order of the Vienna court, and Batthyány officially reprimanded.

But the tide of development in the 1820s and 1830s could no longer be stemmed. Experiments in making porcelain went on at Telkibánya in the well-timbered north of the country, and at Herend, in a district where there were several old-established potteries.

While Telkibánya was supperted by the local londowner Prince Ferdinánd Bretzenheim, Herend was founded by a commoner by the name of Vince Stingl (probably in the mid-1820s, although the documents of the period have been lost.) It is interesting to note that Telkibánya's patron was István Széchenyi, who was a friend of Bretzenheim's, while the experiments at Herend received encouragement from Lajos Kossuth, the other great figure in the period. Just as Széchenyi's influence waned and Kossuth's increased in the years leading up to the 1848 revolution, so the relative importance of the two workshops changed, perhaps not independently of the political developments. Herend won the race to be the pioneer of Hungarian porcelain.

But Herend's importance cannot be explained solely in historical terms. Press reports of the time show that for at least ten years the experiments there had failed to yield satisfactory chinaware that could compete with foreign goods. The pieces were yellowish or greyish. The turning point came when the factory was taken over about 1840 by Mór Fischer. Fischer went to great lengths to obliterate the traces of his predecessor and the earlier experiments, and set 1839 as the date of Herend's foundation. In fact he had plenty of grounds for considering himself the founder.

Stingl can be marked down as a potter who learnt the art of making porcelain, which was more or less generally known by then, but entailed overcoming a number of technical difficulties in practice. But he did not have enough money to buy the equipment he needed, and in the end he had to sell out to the wealthy Fischer, who had been one of his creditors.

Fischer, who enjoyed working on the shopfloor, proved his talent as an entrepreneur as well. Having employed only a handful of people up to then, Herend developed in the 1840s into a workshop capable of production on an

industrial scale. As early as 1841 there were more than 50 employees. Fischer bought various machines and built several new kilns, and for a while continued to employ Stingl and his team, so as not to lose the benefit of their experience. Success came quickly. Early in 1842, Veszprém County Assembly, fired with patriotic zeal, registered Herend's entitlement to use the Hungarian coat of arms as a porcelain factory with imperial and royal privileges. At the Industrial Exhibition later the same year it showed pieces that approached the quality of Viennese porcelain and were acclaimed by the public, including Lajos Kossuth in person.

A serious fire at the factory in 1843 destroyed the early pieces, so that the beginnings og Herend cannot be reconstructed. (Not a single item from the Stingl period survives.) But Fischer was not deterred. He resumed production and entered for the next year's industrial exhibition. As raw material, the factory used the same top-quality precipitated china clay from Zettlitz as the Bohemian porcelain factories, and the workforce, some recruited abroad and some from the local potteries, cleverly tackled the task of imitating the foreign patterns.

The handbooks on Herend tell how the factory began to imitate the products of Meissen, and then those of the other famous European factories like Sèvres, Vienna and Capo di Monte, particularly the ones that had gone out of production. These old Meissen, old Sèvres and old Viennese pieces were doubly successful. In an age before design patents, the Herend mark could be placed on such pieces, which were in short supply and commanded high prices. Aristocratic Hungarian families became regular customers for replacements for pieces from their services that were lost or broken.

So although the establishment of Herend was a milestone in Hungary's bourgeois industrialization and development, its customers were drawn from the Hungarian and foreign aristocracy. At a time when the great European makers were turning to a broader middle-class market, Herend revived the style of the old princely porcelain factories in splendid pieces executed in a masterly fashion. As Fischer himself put it, "The factory set out to adhere in its pattern-making exclusively to the antique, or so-called Old Saxon style, which has come back into favour in recent times."

The greatest influence on Herend was the Late Baroque-Rococo Meissen style of tea and coffee services decorated with flowers, fronds, and often birds. Another debt to Meissen is the woven pattern found on the edges of plates and bowls. The factory concentrated mainly on table services at this time. Small sculptures and vases only came later.

Porcelain being of Chinese origin, Chinese porcelain motifs had always exerted a great influence on the European factories. The use of Chinese and

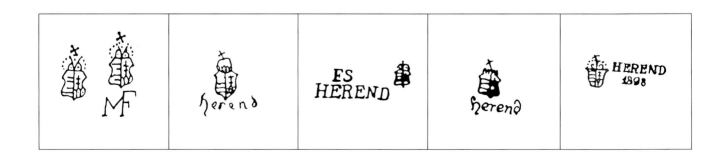

Japanese elements was encouraged by the growing 19th century interest in things Oriental. Herend was no exception, and on seeing the results, the royal Italian court commissioned the factory to replace the pieces missing from its old Chinese porcelain service. This was not an easy assignment, but after more than a year it was accomplished so successfully that the world's premier collection of applied art, the Kensington Museum (now the Victoria and Albert), later bought one such piece under the impression that it was old Persian work.

Herend took part in the Great Exhibition in London in 1851. There were 19 porcelain factories in the Habsburg dominions by that time, but Herend was the only one to win a first prize, among other things for a service decorated with butterflies and flowers. Queen Victoria ordered one, and it came to be known as the Victoria.

Hungary's development into a bourgeois nation-state culminated in the revolution of 1848, but it came to a halt after its defeat in 1849. Hungary lost its shortlived independence, but the march of history could not be halted. Slowly but surely, at a pace hardly perceptible in daily life at the time, the feudal social conditions began to break down in the 1850s and 1860s.

The period between 1851 and 1873 was the heyday of the Herend factory, a decade and a half of prosperity launched by its triumph at the Great Exhibition. The pieces displayed in the Crystal Palace were all sold, and a series of big orders were received. There were about 60 employees at Herend at the time, and although the kilns were renovated and machines installed to mix the material, craft methods were still used for the most part. Not only the painting and throwing were done by hand, but many of the preparatory tasks. This was a sign of underdevelopment at a time when machines were steadily gaining ground in the manufacture of household articles, but Herend managed to turn its deficiency to advantage.

Herend reached its peak in the 1860s at the same time as the Arts and Crafts movement led by Morris and Ruskin declared war on mass-produced factory products, setting out to revive medieval craftsmanship as a way of stemming the tide of shoddy, tasteless goods. Fischer's old-fashioned method of making porcelain to meticulous standards was surprisingly timely, and so was his style, for the mid-19th century was the great period of historical revivals in architecture and the applied arts, with old styles being rediscovered and combined in an eclectic way. Herend did not need to change anything to be up to date; it had been reviving historical styles long before it was fashionable to do so.

Fischer himself has left the most authentic statement of the factory's artistic approach: "For a couple of decades", he says, "the old artistic character

of the shaping (façons) and painting in porcelain manufacture has been lost; instead of these being taken as a yardstick for progressive perfection, artistic creativity has been quite overshadowed, partly by the succession of fashions, partly by changes in tastes. This has occurred in Europe with both the old Sèevres and the Meissen factories, with the cradle of porcelain making, so to speak. So I tried from the outset to gain above all a perfect mastery of the genres of the factories that had gone furthest in their prime. These included the Chinese and Japanese under the Han and Ming dynasties, Sèvres in the age of Louis XV, and Meissen and Frankenthal in the time of Frederic Augustus and Charles Theodore. I was assisted in my undertaking by the fact that many high-ranking lords who were unable to make up the sets of art treasures they had inherited, because of the factory had forsaken the old style, entrusted me with this task... In my patriotic endeavour, however, I have always placed conspicuosly on my products the Hungarian national arms with the letters MF and the name Herend, displaying them with pride. I was encouraged by this success, at the instigation of several art experts and in line with a promise I made to several men of the art world, such as Roy M. and others, at the banquet held on the occasion of the Paris Exposition in 1855, henceforth not to use the modest designation 'after *vieux Sèvres*' or 'after *vieux Saxe*', but to mark my products with the original Herend name: indeed I have cultivated a distinct Herend style for many years and I abide by this consistently. So I believe that if the imitation of some style or other deserves reproof, I may justifiably designate as imitators of Herend the Meissen products that have returned to the old style, indirectly through me."

Fischer has an important message here. Neither historical revival as a school nor the work produced in the spirit of it merely repeats the art of earlier times. Herend pieces, in just the same way, are not variants, however perfect, of the porcelain of Meissen or Sèvres, China or Japan, Vienna or Italy. They are Herend: not divorced from the works that inspired them but not identical with them either. Fischer's adaptation displays, in the way some features are retained, some omitted, some emphasized and some altered, an original taste that is grounded in the winsome, charming, attractive, yet restrained elegance of late Hungarian Biedermeier.

Herend triumphed again at another world exhibition in London in 1862. In the following year Fischer received a knghthood of the Order of Francis Joseph from the emperor, who in 1864 granted him the rights to the patented designs of the imperial porcelain factory, which had closed. So its old rival disappeared, but Herend's reputation in the world went from strength to strength. Another big success came at the 1867 world exposition in Paris, where sales of 83,030 forints were made. (This compares with annual sales in Paris of only

1,000 forints in previous years.) The French court honoured this achievement with particular attention, and soon afterwards Vienna granted Fischer the highest honour a plain citizen could aspire to: a patent of nobility. There were 83 people working at the factory at the time, including 22 painters.

In 1867, the compromise reached between the emperor and the Hungarian politicians who had been in internal or external exile since the end of the war of independence in 1849 turned the Habsburg Empire, in which Hungary had been a hereditary province, a semi-colonial possession of Austria's, into the dual Austro-Hungarian Monarchy. Apart from granting Hungary a high measure of independence, this agreement gave a huge boost to the economy, producing a rate of development unprecedented in Hungarian history.

Another world exhibition opened in Vienna in 1873, and Herend reaped benefits yet again. More interesting in retrospect, perhaps, is the opinion expressed by Jakob Falke, curator of the Museum of Applied Arts in Vienna and a critic of contemporary applied art with a reputation all over Europe: Fischer, he writes, "does not confine himself to copying some famous product or certain types of porcelain; he produces anew what is good and beautiful, and what we admire... Hungary, in my view, should profit more from this factory. With its unique character, it could do the country the same service and occupy the same market as Meissen and Vienna did in their time."

Factories were established in swift succession and the gild system was swept away by the rapid industrialization in the period, but Herend, the pride of Hungary's industrial development, entered a crisis. Behind the overall economic development was a turn towards mechanization and factory production. Herend's archaic style and the high manual input it entailed had become an anachronism. A world economic slump in 1874, along with Fischer's advancing years and the quarrels between his sons, sent the factory into decline. The difficulties were compounded when the firm failed to obtain the credit it needed for development. Fischer had concentrated primarily on the artistic production, rather than commercial exploitation of his great successes (particularly at world exhibitions). He had failed to build up the commercial outlets to provide the flow of orders that could ensure continuity and steady expansion of production. The factory declared itself insolvent in 1874. Although it was discharged two years later, Fischer had to withdraw, and died soon after. His sons took a different line, going in for mass production, but without much success. The factory was bought by the state, which knew it had a duty to preserve it, and then sold again to a joint-stock company. The decision was then taken to produce faience and stoneware as well, in the hope that they would be profitable enough to keep the famous porcelain side going. But this expansion of the factory's range was not a

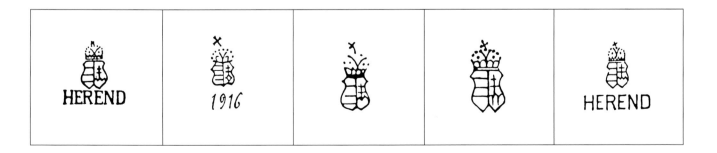

striking success either. The kind of customers on which Herend's strength had rested were dwindling in number, and its foreign markets were lost to cheaper, yet still beautiful and artistic Bohemian porcelain. But the real problem was the failure by Herend's management to spot the trend that was developing in Hungarian applied art, which might have presented big opportunities in what is known today as the fine ceramics industry.

The dissolution of the Austro–Hungarian Monarchy after the First World War dealt Hungary a heavy blow. More than two-thirds of its territory was

The painting workshop in 1924

lost, and reorganization of the economy began with substantially reduced raw-material supplies and commercial scope. Although porcelain manufacture was among the few industries touched only indirectly, Herend felt the effects of the general slump. It had only 23 employees in 1923, when the banks acquired a

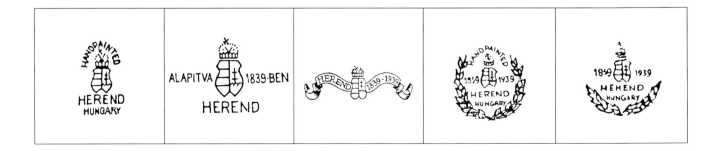

majority of its shares and reorganized the factory financially. Since the type of custom on which its prosperity had been built in the mid-19th century continued to dwindle, Herend was obliged to mark time. A turn for the better came only when the management began to focus on a new market among the lower-middle and middle classes, where there was a demand for relatively small ornamental items at affordable prices. In the 1930s, after the depression was over, the company introduced and developed the production of small sculptures. A range of about 150 small bird and 200 animal figures was

In the worksshop.
A 1943 photograph
by Margit Eitner

produced; figures of numerous famous people were made for china cabinets, and scenes from sport, a newly popular pastime, were captured. This period is associated particularly with the sculptor Ede Telcs. Hired by the factory as an artistic adviser in 1929, he supervised both the reproduction on a reduced scale of work by earlier artists (Miklós Izsó, Adolf Huszár) and the design of new figures by leading masters like Zsigmond Kisfaludi Strobl, János Pásztor, Imre Huszár or the ceramic artist Margit Kovács. Also among the artists commissionded were some accomplished exponents of academic genre sculpture, Jenő Bory, György Vastagh and Éva Vastagh, and several of the

factory's own employees (Tibor Bruck, Jenő Hanzély, Kata Gácser) worked along the same lines. This brought both commercial success—by 1934 the workforce numbered 140 and at the turn of the new decade 450—and professional recognition—a gold medal at the Brussels World Exposition in 1935 and a grand prix in Paris in 1937.

The Second World War was another big setback for the factory. Since it worked to a large extent for export, it was badly affected when it was cut off from its markets in the early 1940s. Nor did peace in 1945 bring an immediate recovery. For years Herend was unable to obtain the china clay it had always imported, and although it experimented with domestic raw materials, they proved suitable only for goods sold on the home market. The situation at Herend returned to normal after nationalization in 1948. A large quantity of mixture was obtained from Limoges, so that exports could be resumed. New workshops were built in the 1950s, and electric kilns installed for firing the decoration. But the shaping and painting continued to be done by hand and wood-fuelled kilns were still used to fire the porcelain, but machines assisted in cleaning and preparing the mixture. So the craft character of production was maintained; only the heavy manual operations were mechanized.

The Hungarian economy was isolated from the rest of the world at this time by the Iron Curtain along its western borders, but there was a demand from the political elite for official gifts, and Herend was well placed to supply this with its ornate and ornamented ware. Not only small figures of Stalin were produced in the Socialist Realist period, but china for workers' tables that recalled (in a more modest way) the tableware of princes and rulers.

Cultural policy changed in the 1960s. The applied arts were no longer expected to convey an ideological position, and Herend regained a measure of commercial and artistic freedom. The change is reflected in the figures. The management consisted in 1949 of one engineer and one technician, whereas in 1963 there were five engineers and ten technicians, along with seven designers. Stepping out into the wide world agin (with orders from as far afield as Australia and the Bahamas), Herend, strange as it may seem, set about creating "new" old patterns to augment its original ones. Two designers, Ágoston Brand and Éva Sz. Horváth, took the lead in this trend towards archaism. They dreamed up the Rococo-style Pompadour, the Empire-style Josephine, the Biedermeier Duna, and even the Neo-Renaissance Beatrix service, although there had been no porcelain manufacturing in Europe at that time, so that one cannot refer in any sense to Renaissance porcelain. Meanwhile the production of figurines was not omitted, and new sculptors (Barna Buza, Pál Pátzay) were recruited for it. From Irén Cs. Illés and László Horváth came a number of services labelled modern, i.e. designs with a stylized

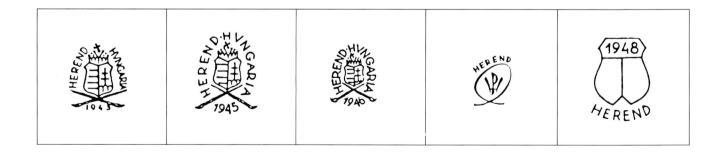

simplicity. In fact Horváth's Saturnus, a service modern in every way, won a prize at the trade's biggest event, at Faenza in Italy. (This was produced commercially, however, by the Alföld Porcelain Factory, not Herend.)

For Herend turned its back on modernity. Since 1976, the factory has run a master course where special training is given to the most talented painters in how to make virtuoso use of the old motifs and style, and there are a great many old-new pieces to show that the objective is a viable one. Herend's critics have reproached it for sticking to its traditions, but history does not run in a straight line. Curiously, the Herend concept is intune with the times again, as it was once before, towards the end of the last century, when its archaism tied in with the historical revivalism of the day. This is an age of eclecticism and post-modernism. The puritan style has given way to rich treatment of surfaces. Ornamentation is no longer considered to be old-fashioned fussiness. The post-modern decorative ware designed by László Horváth, Zoltán Takács, and Ákos Tamás shows that people have realized: Herend has a worthy place in the world.

József Vadas

The Herend showcase at the 1867 World Exposition in Paris

Pictures

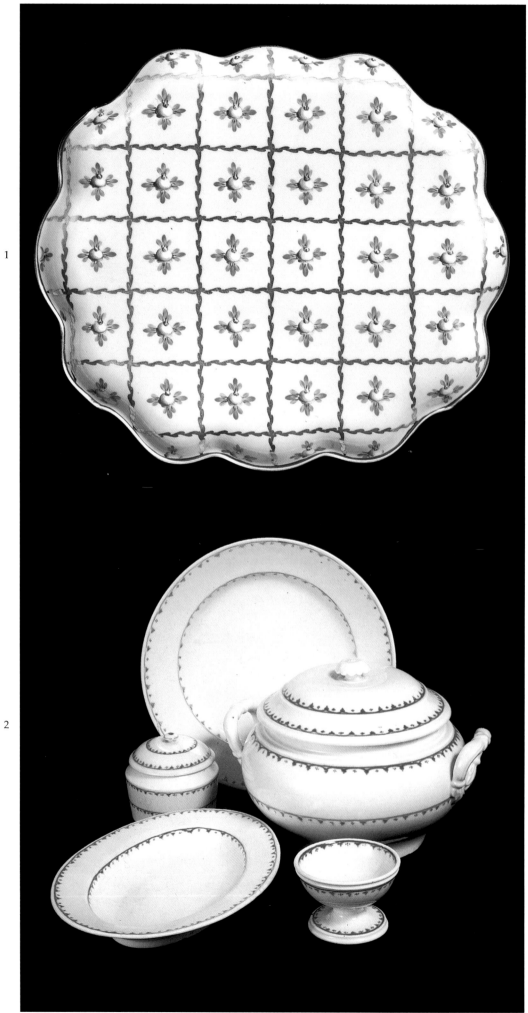

3

4

1. *A tray, part of a smoking set, revived c. 1950–1960 in the "Sèvres Petites roses d'or" pattern*
2. *Dining service, 1840, in "Ranftl Muster", a favourite design of Vienna Porcelain Factory*

3. *Table ornament in openwork with a relief design of floral motifs, c. 1880*
4. *Urn with a lid, replacement for an Empire-style set of Viennese porcelain, c. 1870*

5–6. *An ornamental plate and a detail from the 1840s. The centre shows the 1843 fire at Herend*

7–8. *Ornamental plate and detail, 1861.*
The scene shows Maria Theresa before the Hungarian nobles
in the "Vitam et sanguinem" episode at the Diet of Pozsony

7

8

MORIAMUR PRO REGE NOSTRO!

9

10

11

9–12. *Pieces of the "Füred" service, probably from 1860–1862. The pieces show scenes in and around Balatonfüred, painted in colour and richly gilded*

12

13

13–14. *Ornamental jug and detail, 1846. A rural genre picture with a knight holding a flask, and a pole-well, peasant cottage and shepherd behind*

14

15 ▶

16

15–17. *Ornamental vase and details, 1844,*
with the indented base in Hungarian national
colours and Romantic scenes on the front and back

Rococo Genre Pieces

18

18. *Vase from the turn of the 19th and 20th cc.*
19. *Pot with a lid, a replica of an old piece, made for the 1939 centenary exhibition*
20. *Ornamental vase, 1862*
21. *Jardinière, 1857, decorated with a Watteau scene in a Hungarian landscape*

19

22. *Plate with a Hungarianate genre scene on a blue background, c. 1860*

23

23. *Pieces from a tea service, c. 1860, decorated with French Rococo scenes on a blue background*

24

25

26

24–26. *Plates, c. 1890, with wicker-pattern border and stylized motifs in the mirror*

27. *Detail of a sauce dish with the "Vienna Rose" motif, from the 1840s*
28. *Viennese-style plate with fruit decoration. The original was made in the Fischer period*
29. *Detail of a small bowl, 1858, with "exotic" Oriental decoration painted in purple on the rim*
30. *A cake dish, c. 1870, with a pattern of flowers and birds influenced by Meissen*

"Viktória"

31

32

33

34

35

31–35. *Pieces from a dinner service (1851)*
and a tea service (1860) in "Victoria" pattern

"Queen Victoria": This highly decorative pattern of stylized
blossom branches and butterflies showing Chinese influence
was named after Victoria, Queen of England (1837–1901), who
ordered a service at the Great Exhibition in London in 1851, so
laying the foundations of Herend's international repute

*36–38. Pieces of a dinner service
from the Fischer period*

"Rothschild": This pattern, with naturalistically drawn and painted
birds, pairs and groups, branches and plant ornamentation, took
its name from the famous 19th-c. baronial family of Rothschild,
several branches of which ordered sets in it from Herend

39. *Small dish with a lid, c. 1850, in the "Poissons" design*

"Poissons": This design showing Chinese influence in its depiction and colouring is decorated with stylized fish and seawater plants

39
40

40. *A covered soup tureen from the late 1870's, painted with a so-called "German spray", with a cut lemon knob*

41

42

43

41. *Tray, 1872, with kneeling Chinese servants modelled as handles, painted with "Cubash" pattern in the mirror*
42. *Cup and saucer, c. 1890–1900, with a wicker-relief border, and stylized pomegranate and twigs and scattered flowers as decoration*
43. *A covered bowl painted with animals and flowers in Chinese fashion, 1860*

44

45

46

"Gödöllő"

44. *Tea-service and ornamental pieces, c. 1870*
45. *Saucer, c. 1870*
46. *Cup, c. 1870*
47. *Pieces from a tea service, c. 1880*
48. *Pieces from a tea service, c. 1880*

47

48

"Gödöllő": Re-creation of a rare pattern of the Kakiemon style, brick-red panels alternating with reserves painted with motifs of prunus, bamboo and pine of symbolic significance. Created at Herend for King and Emperor Francis Joseph as a gift for Queen Elizabeth for her palace at Gödöllő. The yellow panelled variant is known as "Siang Jaune"

"Humboldt"

49–53. The "Humboldt" service and its medallions with figures of cherubs holding various musical instruments, before 1857

The medallions on a pink ground with a gilt grid pattern show cherubs holding a music instrument or a book. It was an 88th-birthday present to Alexander Humboldt from the Herend Porcelain Factory

54. *Ornamental vase with a lid, post 1876, with a colourfully painted and gilded Chinoiserie pattern*

55. *A vase in the "Esterházy" pattern, 1857*

"Esterházy": The basic recurrent motif is a white sedge plant on a brick-red or dark green ground. The service was ordered from Herend by a member of the family of Esterházy counts

56. *A pair of ornamental vessels, c. 1870, with decoration showing a Japanese influence and a modelled Fo dog as the handle on the lid*

Chinoiserie

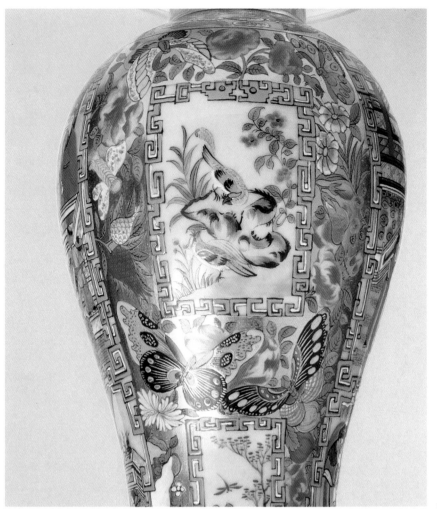

57–59. *Covered ornamental vase with lid,
1856 painted with scenes of Chinese palace
life. Rich gilding and a combination
of Oriental floral motifs and butterflies*

59

Chinoiserie

60. *Ornamental plate, 1874, showing a Chinoiserie garden painted in brick-red and gilt, with Oriental motifs, animals and flowers*
61. *Pieces of a tea and coffee service, 1854, in the "Ming" pattern, designed for King Victor Emanuel of Piedmont and Sardinia*

"Ming": The repeated central motif is a Chinese-style interior with a seated Chinoiserie figure of a woman surrounded by male figures

60

61 ▼

62

▼ 63

62. *Ornamental plate, c. 1895*
63. *Tête-à-tête service, c. 1860*

Chinoiserie

64

65

64. *Tea caddy, c. 1870*
65. *Coffee service, c. 1875*

"Capodimonte"

66. Pieces from a tea service in the "Capodimonte" pattern, 1861
67. Ornamental box, 1870s

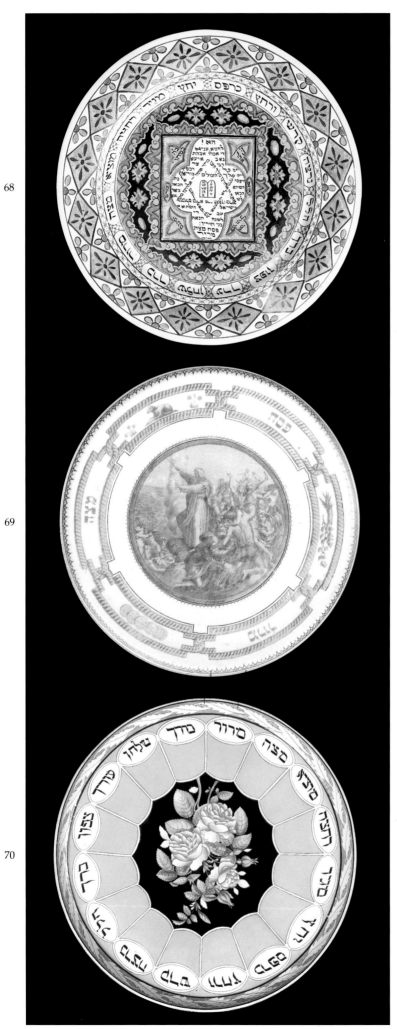

68. *Seder Night plate, c. 1860–1870*
69. *Seder Night plate, c. 1890*
70. *Seder Night plate, perhaps c. 1880*
71. *Chalice, modern*

72–73. Seder Night plate with detail, c. 1870, showing a family celebrating Seder

Neo-Baroque · Neo-Rococo

74. *Ornamental vase, c. 1890, with a cobalt-blue ground, decorated with a richly gilded Neo-Rococo frame surrounding figures against a landscape and a bouquet of roses on the other side*

75. *Ornamental vase, c. 1885, colourfully painted and gilded, decorated with a mythological depiction of Heracles and Omphale on one side and a bouquet of roses on the other*

76. *A pair of ornamental vases and a candlestick, c. 1890–1895, with a cherry-red ground, decorated with a "German floral" spray in a gilt frame*

77

78

79

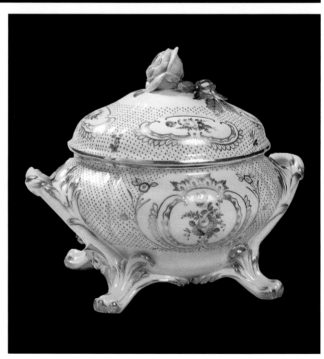

77. *Tea service, 1848*
78. *Fruit basket with a base,*
c. 1890
79. *Covered soup tureen, 1862*
80. *Fruit baskets with bases,*
1874 and early 20th c.
81. *Tea service, perhaps 1843*
or 1848

80

81

Archaism

82. *Pieces from the "Francis Joseph" service, 1899*

83
84

83–84. *Ornamental vases, c. 1900, using pâte-sur-pâte technique, decorated with Sezession-style plant ornamentation*

85
86
87
88

89

90

"Wales": Vessels with exteriors of double lace-like openwork and smooth and often carefully painted inside surfaces, richly gilded and often decorated with colour painting, the handles having a lizard shape. It owes its name to Francis Joseph I, who bought a service at the 1873 Vienna World Exhibition and presented it to the Prince of Wales, later King Edward VII of England (1901–1910)

85. *Tea service in "Wales" pattern c. 1900*
86. *Small bowl in "Wales" pattern, c. 1890–1900*
87. *"Wales" domestic and ornamental pieces of the 1900s*
88. *"Wales" cup with the arms of the Bishop of Veszprém, early 1900s*
89. *Ornamental vessel with Chinoiserie decoration, from the 1890s*
90. *Ornamental vase with a lid, perhaps 1890s*

Ornamental plates

91

92

93

94

91. *Ornamental plate, 1891–1897, with an openwork Neo-Rococo rim and a portrait of a Hungarian nobleman in the centre*

92. *Ornamental plate, 1858, with cherubs fishing painted in the bowl in purple*

93. *Ornamental plate, c. 1860, with a medallion showing a view of Dresden in the middle of the bowl*

94. *Ornamental plate, c. 1860, with a picture of a vineyard owner against a landcape*

95. *Ornamental plate, c. 1870, the centre of the bowl bearing an Oriental-style water scene with animal and plant life*

96. *Ornamental plate, after 1960, with a picture of the Hungarian Parliament*

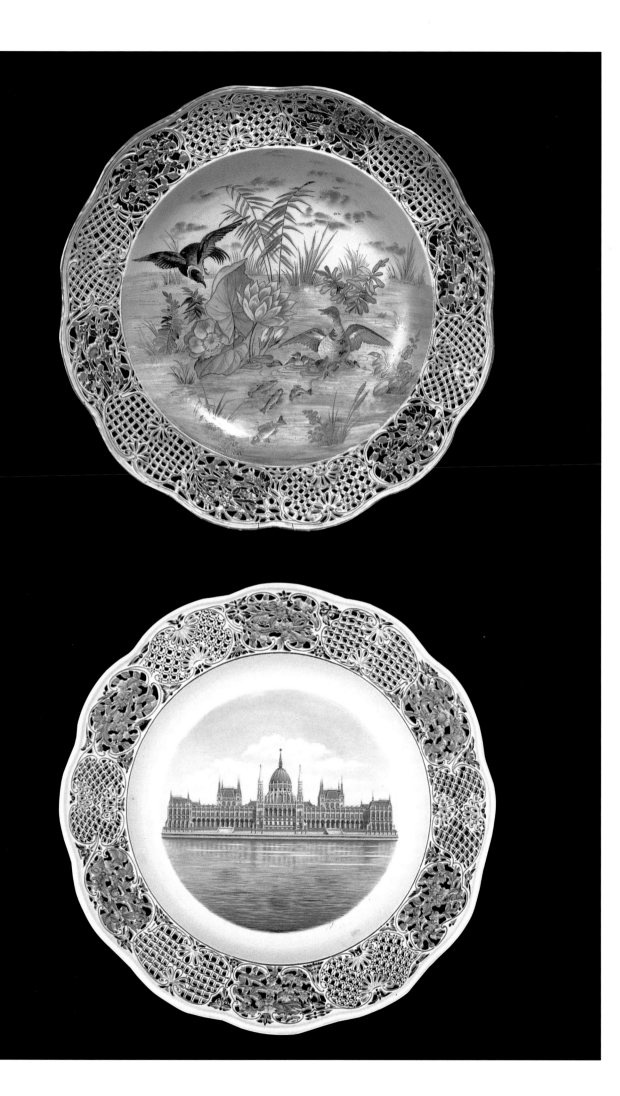

95

96

Statuettes

97

98

99

100

97. *"Mrs Déry", 1930s, designed by Miklós Ligeti*
98. *"Sorrowful Shepherd", perhaps 1930s, modelled*
by Kata Gácser after Miklós Izsó
99. *"Horseherd", 1930s, designed by György Vastagh*

100. *"Hussar Examining His Sword", 1927, designed*
by Zsigmond Kisfaludy Strobl
101. *"Hen", 1880s*
102. *Animal figures, made using models from the 1870s and 1880s*

101

102

103. *"Adam" and "Eve", 1945,*
modelled by Lívia Kuzmik
104. *"Our Lady of Toporc",*
1944, designed by Kata Gácser

New Departures

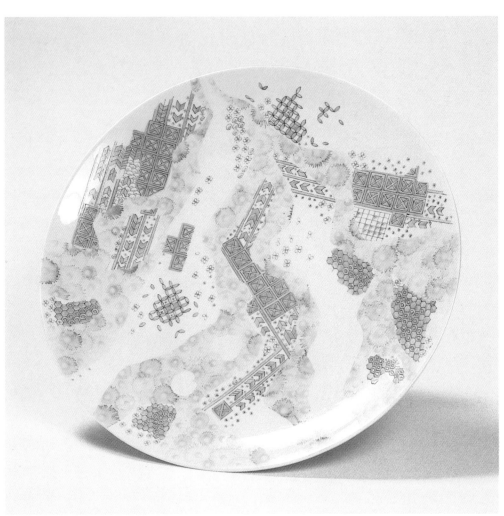

105. *Wall plate "For TMÁ",*
1990, designed by Zoltán Takács
106. *Vases, 1990,*
designed by László Horváth

107

108

*107. Ornamental bowl
and vases, 1990, designed
by Ákos Tamás
108. Openwork bowl and vases,
1990, designed by Ákos Tamás*

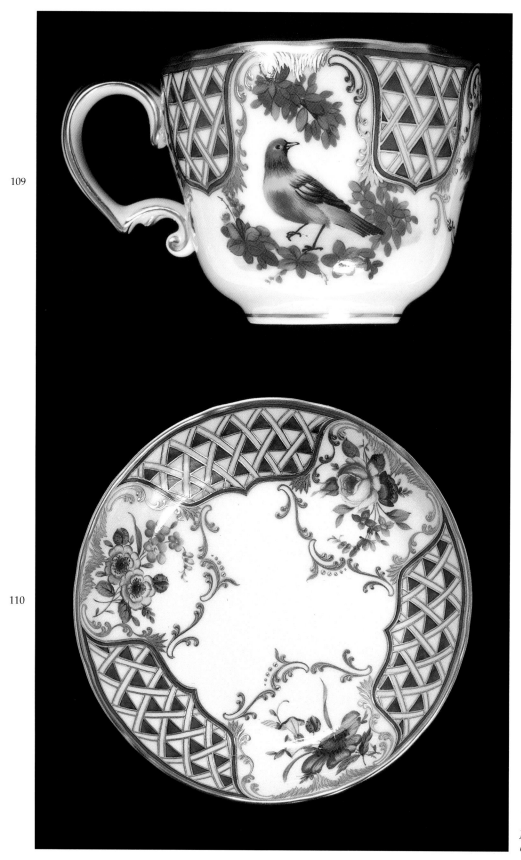

109

110

109–111. *Painting of birds and flowers, with rich raised gilding, evoking the style of Frankenthal*

112–113. *Patterns inspired by the Kakiemon style: "East India Flowers" and "Waldstein"*

14

15 ▶

114. *Vase with a lid, 1988, painted by Miklós Mátis after the motifs of the tapestries from the 1500s in the Cluny Museum*
115. *Vase with a lid, a replica of an original from 1884*

116

117

118

119

116–120. Coffee service, 1971, painted by József Csiszár after 16th-c. Persian miniatures

121. *Dining service in "Dubarry" pattern*

Index of pictures

18. *Ornamental vase*
    "HEREND" embossed on the base, with a hand-drawn
    mark over the glaze and the inscription "Vilmos
    Niermeyer"
    Turn of the 19th and 20th cc.
    A Rococo scene painted in pink with gilt decoration,
    on an Empire-style vase form.
    Herend Museum, Inventory No. MSz. 66.90.01
    Diameter 14.5 cm, height 12 cm

19. *Pot with a lid*
    Replica made for the centenary exhibition in 1939 of
    an early piece from the Mór Fischer period.
    Herend Museum, Inventory No. 66.1138.1
    Height 8.5 cm, diameter 9.5 cm

20. *Ornamental vase*
    The Herend mark of the Hungarian coat of arms
    with a crown on the base, with "1862" and an
    embossed "HEREND"
    1862
    Standing on four voluted, curved gilt legs in the
    shape of acanthus leaves, each side flanked by
    Vienna rose bands on a white ground, with gilt
    framed medallions of a vintage scene and on the
    opposite side a celebration in a wine cellar, and
    goats' heads moulded on each side.
    Herend Museum, Inventory No. 92.3.1
    Height 22 cm

21. *Jardinière*
    The Herend mark of the Hungarian coat of arms
    with a crown on the base, with "857" and the
    painter's number "2"
    1857
    The decoration is on a blue ground; in an oval
    medallion in a richly gilded floral frame is a Watteau
    scene in a Hungarian landscape, with a bouquet of
    flowers and fruits on the opposite side.
    Herend Museum, Inventory No. 79.2100.1
    Height 15 cm, diameter 25 cm

22. *Plate*
    The Herend mark of the Hungarian coat of arms
    with a crown on the base, with "MP"
    c. 1860
    On a blue ground in planes with Neo-Rococo
    framing there are colourful bouquets of flowers, a
    mounted hussar, a horseherd and in the centre a
    genre scene of a horseherd offering a wine skin to a
    shepherd, with a dog sleeping at his feet.
    Budapest Museum of Applied Arts, Inventory No.
    51.1289
    Diameter 14 cm

23. *Pieces from a tea service*
    The Herend mark of the Hungarian coat of arms
    with a crown on the base
    c. 1860
    Herend Museum, Inventory No. 66.446

24–26. *Plates*
    The Herend coat of arms on the base (inscription in
    Gothic script, rubber-stamped)
    c. 1890, 1930s
    Hungarianate decorative motifs on a wicker-pattern
    border, with the whole bowl of the plate covered by
    decoration consisting of stylized pomegranate,
    carnation and tulip motifs made up of archaic,
    Oriental and Hungarianate elements.

Budapest Museum of Applied Arts, Inventory No.
57.512
Herend Museum, Inventory No. 76.2071.a
Diameter 23.5 cm

27. *The "Vienna rose" motif on the base of a sauce dish*
    The monograms "K D" and "T K" on the base
    1840s
    Herend Museum, Inventory No. 66.657.2
    Height 8 cm, rim 15.5 cm

28. *Plate decorated with fruit*
    A faithful replica of an object from the Mór Fischer
    period, a factory sample copy.
    Herend Museum, no inventory no.
    Diameter 26.2 cm

29. *"Exotic", Oriental motif painted in purple on the rim of a
    plate*
    The Herend mark of the Hungarian coat of arms
    with a crown on the base, with "HEREND", "858" and
    the painter's number "10" embossed 1858
    Herend Museum, Inventory No. 63.558
    Diameter 13.5 cm

30. *Dish (for cakes)*
    The Herend mark of the Hungarian coat of arms
    with a crown on the base, with "HEREND" embossed
    c. 1870
    Decoration of flowers and birds showing Meissen
    influence.
    Herend Museum, Inventory No. 63.438
    Diameter 20 cm

31–35. *Pieces of dinner and tea services in "Victoria" pattern*
    On the latter, the Herend mark of the Hungarian
    coat of arms with a crown on the base, with
    "HEREND" and "860" embossed
    1851–1860
    Herend Museum and Budapest Museum of Applied
    Arts

36–38. *Pieces of a dinner service from the Fischer period*
    The pattern was first made for the Vienna Rothschild
    family in the 1860s.
    Herend Museum, Inventory No. 67.1431
    Diameter 29 cm

39. *Small dish with lid*
    The Herend mark of the Hungarian coat of arms
    with a crown on the base
    c. 1880
    The whole surface is decorated with "Poissons"
    pattern.
    Budapest Museum of Applied Arts, Inventory No.
    21 238
    Diameter 15 cm, height 12 cm

40. *Covered soup tureen*
    The Herend mark of the Hungarian coat of arms
    with a crown on the base, with "HEREND" and "S"
    embossed
    After 1876
    Decorated with a "German spray" of flowers, with a
    modelled half-lemon and lemon slice as the handle
    of the lid.
    Budapest Museum of Applied Arts, Inventory No.
    54.363
    Diameter 20.5 cm, height 12 cm

41. *Tray*
    The Herend mark of the Hungarian coat of arms
    with a crown on the base, with "HEREND" and "1872"
    embossed

1872
An openwork rim, decorated on each side with modelled Chinoiserie figures, an oval body, "Cubash" decoration.
Budapest Museum of Applied Arts, Inventory No. 54.360
Diameter 25.5 cm, height 10 cm

42. *Cup and saucer*
A green ribbon-and-crown mark on the base with an embossed "HEREND"
c. 1890–1990
A rim bordered by a gold line, wavy with a wicker pattern, and pomegranate and Hungarianate decoration.
Budapest Museum of Applied Arts, Inventory No. 56.268
Diameter of cup 6.5 cm, diameter of saucer 11.5 cm, height 4.5 cm

43. *Covered bowl*
The Herend mark of the Hungarian coat of arms with a crown on the base, with "M F" and "860"
1860
Painted in Chinese fashion with animal and plant life, with modelled handles on each side.
Budapest Museum of Applied Arts, Inventory No. 52.2245
Diameter 24 cm, height 14 cm

44. *Tea service and ornamental pieces*
The Herend mark of the Hungarian coat of arms with a crown on the base
c. 1870
Herend Museum, Inventory No. 66.351

45. *Saucer in "Siang Jaune"*
The Herend mark of the Hungarian coat of arms with a crown on the base
c. 1870
Herend Museum, Inventory No. 83.951.1

46. *Cup in "Gödöllő" pattern*
The Herend mark of the Hungarian coat of arms with a crown on the base
c. 1870
Herend Museum, Inventory No. 66.352.1

47. *Pieces from a tea service in "Gödöllő" pattern*
The Herend mark of the Hungarian coat of arms with a crown on the base
c. 1880
Herend Museum

48. *Tea service in "Gödöllő" pattern*
The Herend mark of the Hungarian coat of arms with a crown on the base
c. 1880
Budapest Museum of Applied Arts, Inventory No. 1490–1494

49–52. *The medallions of the "Humboldt" service with figures of cherubs and various instruments*

53. *The "Humboldt" service*
The Herend mark of the Hungarian coat of arms with a crown on the base
Before 1857
A present from the Herend Porcelain Factory to Alexander Humboldt on his 88th birthday. A gilt grid on a pink ground, with medallions showing cherubs holding a musical instrument and a book.
Herend Museum, Inventory No. 67.760

54. *Covered ornamental vase*
The Herend mark of the Hungarian coat of arms with a crown on the base, with "HEREND" and "S" embossed
After 1876
Decorated with colourfully painted and gilded Chinoiserie.
Herend Museum, Inventory No. 63.61.01
Diameter 14.9 cm, height 60.5 cm

55. *Vase in "Esterházy" pattern*
The Herend mark of the Hungarian coat of arms with a crown on the base, with "HEREND", "1857" and painter's number "30" embossed
1857
Herend Museum, Inventory No. 1651
Height 26 cm, diameter 10 cm

56. *Pair of ornamental vessels with lids*
The Herend mark of the Hungarian coat of arms with a crown embossed on the base
c. 1870
The cobalt-blue ground under the glaze and the motifs of the colourful painting and gilding over the glaze show the influence of Japanese Arita (Imari) ware; the lid handles are modelled Fo dogs.
Budapest Museum of Applied Arts, Inventory No. 1569
Height 66 cm, rim 17 cm

57–59. *Ornamental vase with lid*
The Herend mark of the Hungarian coat of arms with a crown on the base, with "1856", painter's number "2", and "R" (?)
1856
Decorated with a colourfully painted and gilded Chinoiserie scene, with Oriental motifs, animal and plant life.
Budapest Museum of Applied Arts, Inventory No. 1583
Height 29.5 cm

60. *Ornamental plate in "Miramare" pattern*
The Herend mark of the Hungarian coat of arms with a crown on the base, with "1856", painter's number "2", and "R" (?)
1856
Decorated with a Chinoiserie garden and building, painted in brick-red and gilt.
Budapest Museum of Applied Arts, Inventory No. 1459
Diameter 34.5 cm

61. *Pieces of a tea and coffee service in "Ming" pattern*
The Herend mark of the Hungarian coat of arms with a crown on the base, with "HEREND" embossed and the inscription "1854 Herendi Gyár tavaszkor" (Herend Factory Spring 1854) in black
Colourfully painted with Chinoiserie female figures and scenes.
Herend Museum, Inventory No. 69.2013.1

62. *Ornamental plate*
A crown-and-ribbons mark on the base under the glaze
Decoration painted in blue under the glaze and rust-red over the glaze in the style of Japanese Arita (Imari) porcelain.
Budapest Museum of Applied Arts, Inventory No. 64.152
Diameter 51.5 cm

63. *Tête-à-tête service*
The Herend mark of the Hungarian coat of arms with a crown on the bases
c. 1860
Decorated with colourfully painted and gilded Chinoiserie landscapes and scenes.
Budapest Museum of Applied Arts, Inventory No. 53.1322.1-5

64. *Tea caddy*
"HEREND" embossed the base
c. 1870
Four curved containers for tea fit onto the round balustered tray, with a cockerel on each of the necks. The Chinese figure on the cylindrical central piece holds a small tray.
Budapest Museum of Applied Arts, Inventory No. 14 839.a-d

65. *Coffee service*
Herend Porcelain Factory; the Herend mark of the Hungarian coat of arms with a crown on the bases, with "75"
c. 1875
Decorated all over with scattered flowers in Japanese taste; the feet and handles are formed into leafy fronds.
Budapest Museum of Applied Arts, Inventory No. 1516–1520

66. *Pieces of a tea service in "Capodimonte" pattern*
"HEREND", "MF", "1861" and "18" (perhaps a painter's number) embossed on the bases.
1861
Naturalistically painted with oval medallions and a gilt frame, with tiny flowers.
Budapest Museum of Applied Arts, Inventory No. 54.310, 53.310, 21 253

67. *Ornamental box in "Capodimonte" pattern*
The Herend mark of the Hungarian coat of arms with a crown gilded on the base
1870s
Budapest Museum of Applied Arts, Inventory No. 18.333

68. *Seder Night plate*
"HEREND" embossed on the base
c. 1860–1870
Budapest Museum of Applied Arts, Inventory No. 55.676
Diameter 30 cm, height 3 cm

69. *Seder Night plate*
Work of a Herend painter on a piece of uncertain origin
c. 1890 (?)
Herend Museum, Inventory No. 67.1212.1
Diameter 34.8 cm, height 3 cm

70. *Seder Night plate*
Herend Porcelain Factory, the Herend mark of the Hungarian coat of arms with a crown on the base, with "HEREND" embossed
c. 1880
Chinese-style flowers on a black ground in the centre of the bowl.
Herend Museum, Inventory No. 66.391.2
Diameter 36 cm, height 3 cm

71. *Chalice*
Foliage decoration on a white ground
Modern piece

72–73. *Seder Night plate*
c. 1870 (?)
In a framed field in the centre of the bowl, a family celebrating Seder.
Herend Museum, Inventory No. 67.1535.1
Diameter 36.5 cm, height 3 cm

74. *Ornamental vase*
The Herend mark of the Hungarian coat of arms with a crown on the base
c. 1890
Figures against a landscape in a richly gilt Neo-Rococo frame on a cobalt-blue ground, with a bouquet of roses on the other side. The handles are modelled goats' heads.
Herend Museum, Inventory No. 66.1935
Height 29.5 cm

75. *Ornamental vase*
The Herend mark of the Hungarian coat of arms with a crown on the base, with "HEREND" in Gothic script
c. 1885
Colourfully painted adn gilded, and decorated with a mythological depiction of Heracles and Omphale, and a bouquet of roses on the reverse side. The handles spring from modelled oak leaves.
Budapest Museum of Applied Arts, Inventory No. 62.1592
Height 61 cm

76. *Pair of ornamental vases and candlestick*
The crown-and-ribbons Herend mark on the bases in black
c. 1890–1895
"German sprays" of flowers in gold frames on a cherry-red ground.
Budapest Museum of Applied Arts, Inventory No. 16 961, 16 962, 16 963
Heights 36 cm and 59 cm

77. *Tea service*
"F M HEREND 848" embossed on the base of the cup
1848
Scale decoration around a gilt rim with flowers and garlands scattered over the bodies.
Herend Museum, no inventory no.

78. *Fruit basket with base*
Blue crown-and-ribbons Herend mark on the base
c. 1890
Modelled based with rocaille motifs, a wicker body with two handles, and relief purple floral and leaf motifs in the wicker.
Herend Museum, Inventory No. 66.223
Height 27 cm

79. *Covered soup tureen*
The Herend mark of the Hungarian coat of arms with a crown on the base, with "862"
1862
Decorated with coloured "German sprays" of flowers in rocaille frames and dotted in green; the handles and feet are modelled like acanthus leaves.
Museum of Applied Arts, Inventory No. 52.3834
Diameter 20 cm, height 26 cm

80. *Fruit baskets with bases*
The Herend mark of the Hungarian coat of arms with a crown on the bases, with "HEREND" embossed, and in the case of the piece under Inventory No. 1565, "1874"
1874 and early 20th c.

A basket with two handles on a modelled base of rocaille motifs, with relief blue flowers with green leaves and "German sprays" of flowers on the wicker. The piece under Inventory No. 1565 has two angels playing with doves on the bottom of the basket.
Budapest Museum of Applied Arts, Inventory No. 1565, 51.1396

81. *Pieces of a tea service*
"F M HEREND 848 (?), 843 (?)" embossed on the bases
1843, 1848
Scale ornamentation around the gilt rims, with tiny flowers scattered over the bodies.
Budapest Museum of Applied Arts, Inventory No. 16.341

82. *Pieces from the "Francis Joseph" service made for the king*
The Herend mark of the Hungarian coat of arms with a crown on the base, with "HEREND" and "1899" embossed
1899
Herend Museum, Inventory No. 66.1985.1

83. *Ornamental vases*
Designed by Jenő Farkasházy, with "HEREND" embossed on the bases
c. 1900
Decorated with sedge or lilies using pâte-sur-pâte technique, in Sezession style.
Herend Museum, Inventory No. 59.391, MSz. 63.41.01
Height 48.8 cm, diameter 11.7 cm

84. *Vases*
Herend Porcelain Factory, with "HEREND" embossed on the bases
c. 1900
Decorated with Sezession-style plant ornamentation using pâte-sur-pâte technique.
Herend Museum, Inventory No. 63.38.01, 63.37.2, 66.1937.1, 63.72.1
Diameters 8.4 cm, 7.8 cm, 10 cm, heights 26 cm, 22 cm, 23.3 cm

85. *Pieces of a tea service in "Wales" pattern*
The Herend mark of the Hungarain coat of arms with a crown under the glaze on the base
c. 1900
Double grid-like openwork sides, with gilt rosettes, the lid handles modelled as dragons, painted blue and gilded.
Herend Museum, Inventory No. 66.375

86. *Small bowl in "Wales" pattern*
The Herend mark of the Hungarain coat of arms with a crown under the glaze on the base
c. 1890–1900
Double openwork body, with gilt rosettes; a stylized gilt garland of flowers on a lilac band inside the vessel.
Budapest Museum of Applied Arts, Inventory No. 71.6
Height 5.5 cm, diameter 15 cm

87. *Domestic and ornamental pieces in "Wales" pattern*
Herend Porcelain Factory, the Herend mark of the Hungarian coat of arms with a crown on the bases, with "HEREND" embossed
Herend Museum, no inventory no.

88. *"Wales" cup with the arms of the Bishop of Veszprém*
Herend Porcelain Factory, the Herend mark of the Hungarian coat of arms with a crown on the base
Early 1900s
Herend Museum, Inventory No. 66.98
Height 10 cm

89. *Ornamental vessel*
A green crown-and-ribbons mark and embossed "HEREND" on the base 1890s
The shape follows an Oriental prototype in the form of an ornamental gourd, with Chinoiserie decoration.
Herend Museum, Inventory No. 66.1930

90. *Ornamental vase with lid*
1890s (?)
An openwork body with an amorette scene in an oval frame and goats' heads as handles.
Herend Museum, Inventory No. 6727

91. *Ornamental plate*
The Herend mark of the Hungarian coat of arms with a crown on the base, with "HEREND" embossed
Between 1891 and 1897
Openwork Neo-Rococo rim, a portrait of a Hungarian nobleman in the bowl.
Herend Museum, Inventory No. 63.190.1
Diameter 25.5 cm

92. *Ornamental plate*
The Herend mark of the Hungarian coat of arms with a crown on the base with "HEREND" and painter's number "6"
1858
Openwork Neo-Rococo rim, with cherubs fishing painted in purple in the bowl
Herend Museum, Inventory No. 92.5.1
Diameter 25.5 cm

93. *Ornamental plate*
"HEREND" embossed in the base, along with "DRESDEN" in black
c. 1860
Openwork Neo-Rococo rim, then lavish gilt ornamentation on a dark blue ground, and a medallion with a view of Dresden in the centre of the bowl.
Herend Museum, Inventory No. 92.1.1
Diameter 25.5 cm

94. *Ornamental plate*
"HEREND" and "F M" embossed on the base
c. 1860
Openwork Neo-Rococo rim, with a medallion of a vineyard owner against a landscape framed in lacy gilding that almost completely masks the dark blue ground.
Herend Museum, Inventory No. 92.2.1
Diameter 25.5 cm

95. *Ornamental plate*
"HEREND" embossed on the base
c. 1870
Openwork Neo-Rococo rim, with an Oriental-style water scene with animal and plant life in the bowl.
Herend Museum, Inventory No. 66.285.1
Diameter 51.5 cm

96. *Ornamental plate*
After 1960
Openwork Neo-Rococo rim, with a picture of the Hungarian Parliament in the bowl
Herend Museum, Inventory No. 92.6.1
Diameter 25.5 cm

97. *"Mrs Déry"*
Designed by Miklós Ligeti
1930s
The statuette shows the actress with a lute.
Herend Museum, Design No. 5753
Height 35 cm

98. *"Sorrowful Shepherd"*
Modelled by Kata Gácser after Miklós Izsó's statue.
1930s (?)
Herend Museum, Design No. 5427

99. *"Horseherd"*
Designed by György Vastagh
1930s (?)
Herend Museum, Design No. 5888

100. *"Hussar Examining His Sword"*
Designed by Zsigmond Kisfaludi Strobl
1927
Herend Museum, Design No. 5505
Height 38 cm

101. *"Hen"*
The Herend mark of the Hungarian coat of arms with a crown on the base, with "S"
1880s
Herend Museum, Inventory No. 62.3

102. *Animal figures*
New pieces made using the original models from the 1870s and 1880s

103. *"Adam" and "Eve"*
On the base both the "new" blue and the embossed Herend mark of the Hungarian coat of arms with a crown, "1945", and "15711" and "15710" respectively
Modelled by Lívia Kuzmik.
Budapest Museum of Applied Arts, Inventory No. 62.238, 62.239
Height 33.5 cm

104. *"Our Lady of Toporc"*
On the base the new "blue" Herend mark and "1944", with "HEREND 5632" embossed
Designed by Kata Gácser.
Budapest Museum of Applied Arts, Inventory No. 61.230
Height 54.5 cm

105. *Wall plate "For TMÁ"*
On the base the new "blue" Herend mark, and underneath "Designed by Takács Zoltán" (the name in Italics), then "80388 (TMÁ)" denoting Mrs Ágnes Matejovszky Takács, and an embossed "HEREND"
1990
Shaped on the wheel, decorated with matt, lively, spiral, decisive movements with a paint gun, then touched up with brush or pen, on a glossy white glaze. The motifs include tiny flowers, arrows, honeycomb cells, stars, snails and leaves.
Design No. 7543
Budapest Museum of Applied Arts, Inventory No. 91.8
Diameter 38.5 cm

106. *Vases*
On the bases the "new" blue Herend mark, an embossed "HEREND", then "Designed by Horváth László" (the name in Italics) and the artist's dated signature in grey-silver lustre paints
1990
"Studio" work, the surface colourless inside with a matt glaze, the outside cobalt nitrate, treated with wax, painted with lustre paints, fired several times and with a matt glaze. The motifs are geometricized, and the dominant colours orange, lilac, blue-grey and silver.
Budapest Museum of Applied Arts, Inventory No. 91.1, 91.2, 91.3
Heights 34.5 cm, 26 cm, 24 cm

107. *Ornamental bowl and vases*
On the bases the new "blue" Herend mark, with "HEREND TAMÁS ÁKOS" embossed, and underneath "Designed by Tamás Ákos" (the name in Italics)
1990
"Studio" work, the title of the bowl is "Coral" and of one of the vases "Strato". The vessels are made from white, grey, blue-grey, ochre and pink-coloured clays, with an intermittent matt glaze.
Budapest Museum of Applied Arts, Inventory No. 91.13, 91.14, 91.16
Heights 13 cm, 31 cm, 31 cm

108. *Openwork bowl and vases*
On their bases the new "blue" Herend mark, with "HEREND TAMÁS ÁKOS" embossed, and underneath "Designed by Tamás Ákos" (the name in Italics)
1990
"Studio" work, the vessels are made from clays in white, three shades of grey, and pink, in squeezed stripes, with a matt clay-like surface.
Budapest Museum of Applied Arts, Inventory No. 91.11, 91.15, 91.17
Heights 13 cm, 35 cm, 29 cm

109–111. *Revived coffee service in Frankenthal style*

112–113. *Inspired by the Kakiemon style: "East India Flowers" and "Waldstein"*

114. *Vase with a lid*
1988
Painted by Miklós Mátis
The decoration is based on the motifs of the tapestries from the 1500s in the Cluny Museum.
Herend Porcelain Factory

115. *Ornamental vase with a lid*
Revival of an original made in 1884 with some altered decoration.
Height 60.5 cm

116–120. *Coffee service*
1971
Painted by József Csiszár after 16th-c. Persian miniatures.

121. *"Dubarry" dinner service*

UDVARRÉSZLET

ÖNTŐMŰHELY

FESTÉSZET